EMERGING
VOICES

Clear the Track

Andy Brooke

Cambiata (opt. div.), baritone, and piano

DIFFICULTY LEVEL ●●○

OXFORD

Clear the Track

Trad. sea shanty
arr. ANDY BROOKE

¹ *clipper* = a fast, 19th-century sailing ship that carried passengers, freight, and/or mail
² *Margaret Evans* = a clipper built in 1846 that was part of the *Black Cross Line* shipping company's fleet,
who operated between Britain and America

Duration: 3 mins

[3] *bulgine* = a steam engine, built for power not speed, that carried freight up and down the dockside; its name is thought to be a portmanteau of 'bull' and 'engine'
[4] *low-backed car* = a simple carriage or trailer

*Either or both cambiata parts may be sung.

6

* Small notes are for rehearsal only.

snapping out of it

Tempo I

ISBN 978-0-19-356025-3

Music originated by Andrew Jones
Printed in England by Halstan & Co. Ltd, Amersham, Bucks.